THIS
LITTLE
PEBBLE

Franklin Watts
First published in Great Britain in 2016 by The Watts Publishing Group

Credits
Editor: Julia Bird
Designer: Jeni Child

HB ISBN 978 1 4451 4969 1
PB ISBN 978 1 4451 4968 4

Printed in China

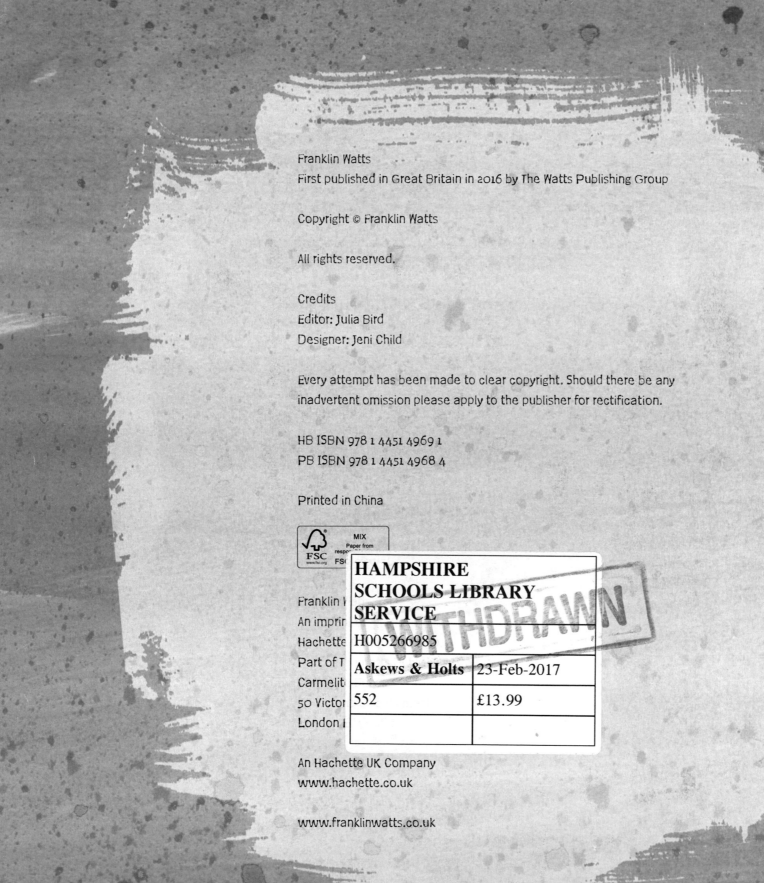

Franklin W...
An impri...
Hachette...
Part of T...
Carmelit...
50 Victor...
London ...

An Hachette UK Company
www.hachette.co.uk

www.franklinwatts.co.uk

A LOOK AT ROCK CYCLES

THIS LITTLE PEBBLE

Anna Claybourne

Illustrated by
Sally Garland

W

FRANKLIN WATTS
LONDON•SYDNEY

CONTENTS

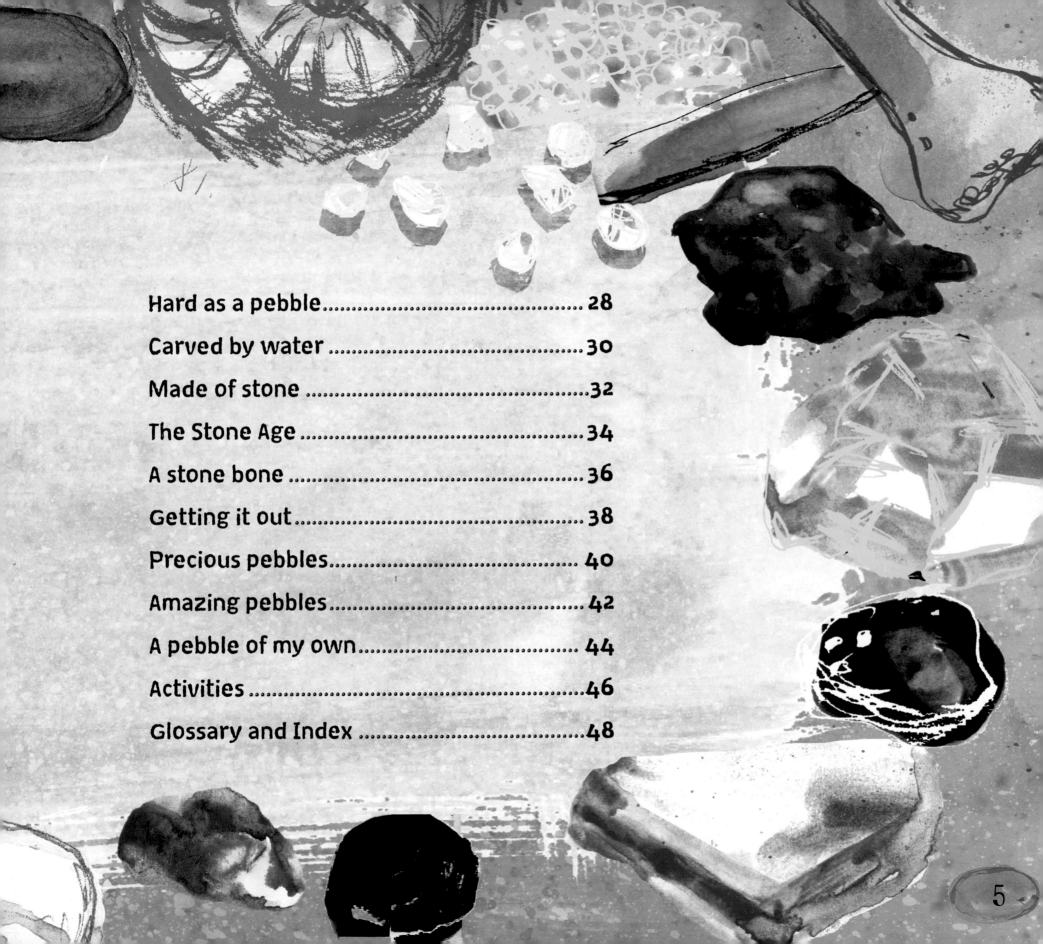

THIS LITTLE PEBBLE

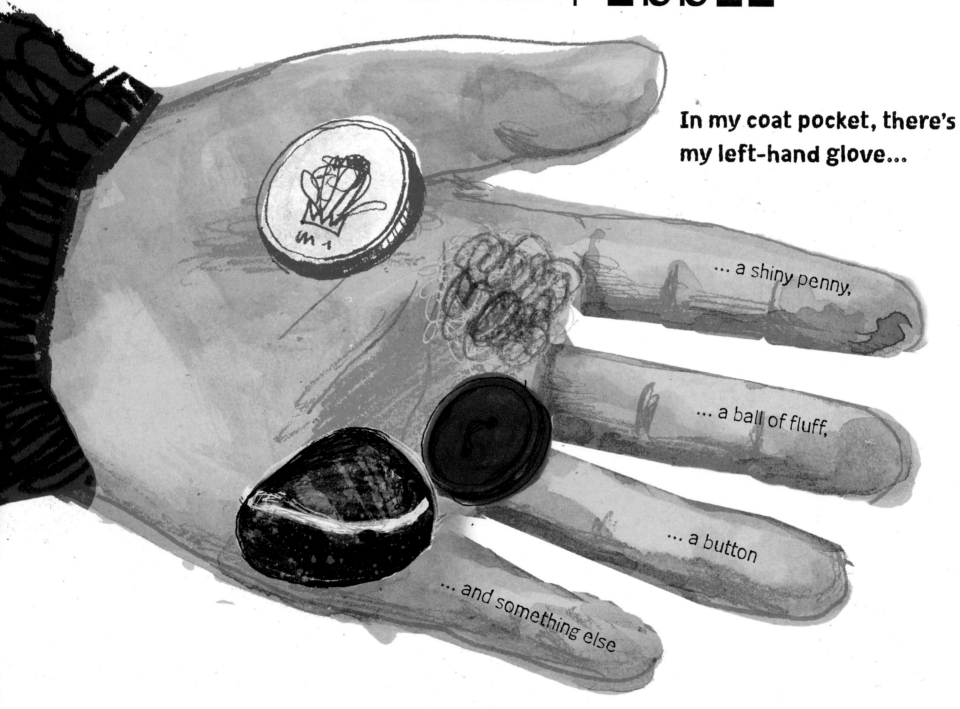

In my coat pocket, there's my left-hand glove...

... a shiny penny,

... a ball of fluff,

... a button

... and something else

. . . a smooth, hard, grey, oval pebble.

6

I hold it in my hand.
It's small, but heavy.
The smooth, dry stone is cool.
I turn it around and around.
What kind of stone is my pebble made of?
Could it be precious?

How did it end up in the stream,
by the campsite,
next to the woods,
where I found it,
long ago last summer?

What made it this shape?
And HOW did it get
that stripe?

Where did my pebble
come from? How did it—
end up like this?

ROCKS ARE EVERYWHERE!

Whenever you explore outside, it's not that hard to find a pebble. They're everywhere!

How DID all those pebbles get there?

Pebbles come from rocks. That's what they are made of. And our world is mostly made of rocks too!

Mountains, cliffs, crags, boulders, sandy deserts and stony beaches – they are all made of rocks.

8

Rock can come in big chunks,
like a cliff or mountain.
Or as smaller boulders.
Or as little pebbles, like mine.
Even the soil contains pebbles and grains of stone.
How many pebbles are there in the whole world?

There must be **billions!**

9

THE WORLD IS A PEBBLE

In fact, our planet, the Earth, is one ginormous pebble.

It's much bigger than my pebble, of course. But it's basically a smooth, round ball of rock, **zooming** through space.

Ice
Ice covers the coldest places.

City
There are cities and towns on top too.

Soil

Lots of the Earth's rocky land is covered in soft, crumbly soil, grass, plants and trees.

Desert

There's not much soil in a desert, so it's easy to see the rock.

Hills

In some places the rock sticks up, making cliffs, hills or mountains.

Seas

Where the rock is lowest down, it's covered in water – the sea!

THE MOON IS A ROCK TOO.

You can't always see the rock, as it's covered up with soil, water, grass and trees, farms or houses.

But it's there underneath these things, all over the world.

GOING DOWN...

If you could dig down under the ground,
what would you find?

Start digging...

Down, down through the soil...
it's about as deep
as a room in my house.

Deeper and
deeper . . .

CRUNCH!

I've hit bedrock
– the hard rock under the soil.

The deeper you go, the HOTTER it gets...

Deep, deep down,
it's really hot!

The rock isn't hard any more
– it's gooey, melted magma.

JIGSAW PIECES

The Earth has a crust of hard rock...
but it's not just one big piece.

It's made up of giant rock sections,
called plates.
They fit together like jigsaw pieces.

The ground seems to stay still...
but it doesn't!
The plates slowly move around,
squeeeeze and CRUNCH
against each other.

CRUNCH!

14

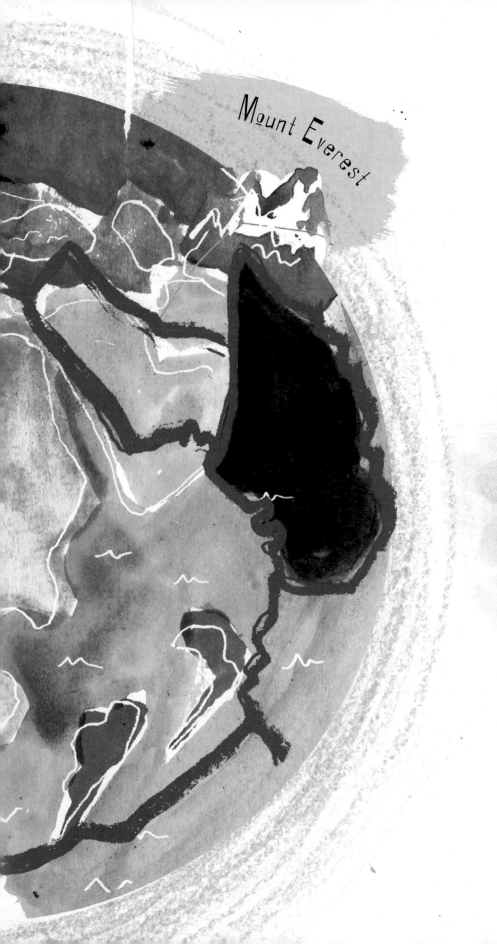

Mount Everest

The pushing plates can make rocky land
SCRUNCH together and pile up.
That makes mountains.

Squeezing plates made the
Himalayan Mountains, and
the world's highest mountain,
Mount Everest.

Still growing!
The plates are still squeezing against
each other and pushing the Himalayas up.
They grow about 1 cm higher every year.
That's about as slowly as my toenails grow!

15

EARTHQUAKES

Mostly, the Earth's plates move ve-e-ery slowly.

But sometimes, as they are moving, they get caught on each other.
The plates push harder, and harder, and harder...

... until suddenly, they slip.

This makes the ground
shake, jump or crack
open suddenly.

It's an
EARTHQUAKE!

16

Buildings fall down...

QUICK! Get out!

Soil, pebbles and mud crash
down slopes...

Landslide!

Earthquakes are SO strong,
some rocks get torn apart.

Others get squashed
and scrunched together.

17

OUT OF THE VOLCANO

**Inside the Earth, the rock is hot, melted magma.
Sometimes, it gets out... and that makes a volcano!**

Magma pushes up into the crust from below.
It comes close to the surface...

and once in a while, it bursts right through!

...BOOM!

The volcano is
erupting!

Sometimes, magma
EXPLODES
out of the ground with a big bang.

Sometimes, it just flows out gently.
Once it has come out,
the melted rock is called lava.

It's hot... REALLY hot!

Hotter than a
boiling kettle.

Hotter than a
roasting oven.

Then the lava cools down,
and goes hard.

It makes rocky lumps,
boulders...

...and little,
brand-new
pebbles!

19

WEARING AWAY

Rocks and pebbles seem so solid and hard. They seem as if they will last forever. But they change all the time.

Once upon a time, my pebble was not small, smooth and round. It was part of a bigger piece of rock –

a cliff, crag or boulder.

Maybe my pebble was somewhere in here.

Thanks to wind, rain, ice and time,
a piece of rock broke off.

It rolled downhill,
and into a stream.

It got jumbled and tumbled
along with all the other pebbles,
and its corners got worn away.

It ended up smooth, round,
and just the right size to
fit in my hand.

21

A HANDFUL OF SAND

Look at sand through a magnifying glass, and what do you see?

Sand is made of **tiny, tiny pebbles,** just like my pebble, but much smaller!

Sand is made of rocks that have worn away and broken into little pieces. As they rub against each other, the grains of sand become smoother and rounder.

On beaches, waves help to make sand as they crash against rocks and wear them away.

In deserts, wind wears away rocks into pebbles and sand.

Back to stone!

Sand sinks into the sea and down,
down to the bottom.

It collects in layers,
one on top of the other.

The sand at the bottom gets
squeezed and squashed down —
until it sticks together.
It turns back into solid stone.
It's called sandstone!

23

ROUND AND ROUND

What happens to old rocks?
They turn into new rocks. They go around and around,
changing from one rock into another.

Rocks wear away and turn into sand or mud.

New rocks form from squashed-down sand or mud.

Sandstone forms from sand

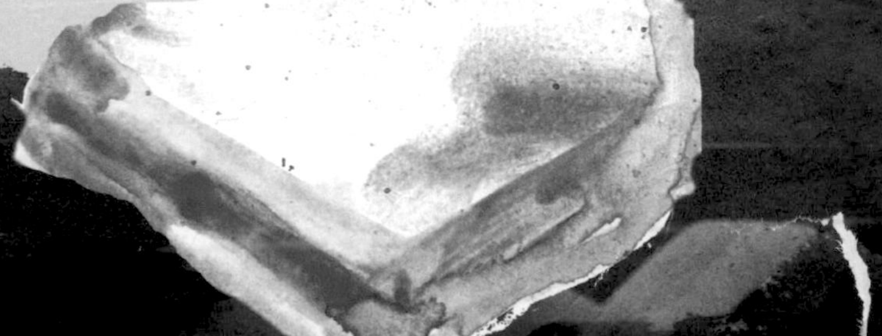

Shale forms from mud

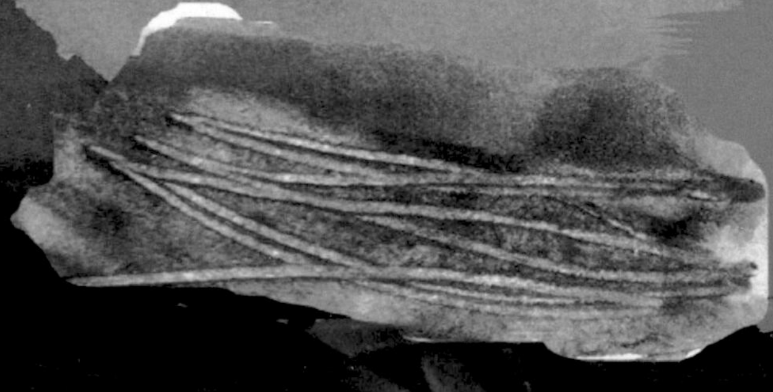

Melted rock from inside the Earth bursts out of volcanoes.

It cools and forms new types of hard rock.

Obsidian

Pumice

Rocks get squashed hard by earthquakes and moving plates.

As the rock gets squashed, it changes into different rock.

Marble

Slate

WHICH IS WHICH?

How many different pebbles have you found?
They come in all kinds of shapes and colours.

Brown siltstone

Pebbles are made of different rocks and minerals.
That's why they look and feel different.

How many types are there altogether?

Thousands!

Grey
limestone

What about my pebble?

My pebble is grey, oval, flattish, and smooth – but not shiny.

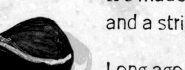

It's made of limestone rock
and a stripe of calcite mineral.

Long ago, my pebble was part
of a rock with a crack in it.

The white calcite filled in the crack.

The rock broke up into pebbles.

Striped
gneiss

Rough
greywacke

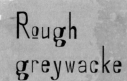

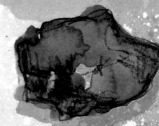

Speckled granite

White
chalk

Pink
feldspar

Round basalt

Smooth mudstone

Flat slate

Black jet

Yellow amber

See-through quartz

Shiny flint

HARD AS A PEBBLE

You might hear people say something is 'rock hard'.
But not all rocks are hard! They can be very hard
— or soft, crumbly and easy to break.

Diamond is a super-hard mineral
— one of the hardest on Earth.

Granite is a
very hard rock.

My pebble is pretty hard too. I can throw it on the ground,
jump on it, kick it and it doesn't break.

Drawing with rocks

But if a rock is soft enough you can draw with it. It makes a mark, made of tiny bits of the rock crumbling off.

My coloured chalks are made of soft chalk rock, mixed with dye.

There's a soft mineral called graphite in pencils, too.

CARVED BY WATER

Water seems softer than rock. It flows, and you can put your hand through it.

But soft, runny water
can cut right through rock!

A stream or river flows along,
washing away soil and plants.

Slowly, slowly, the rushing water
wears away the rock underneath, too.

A river can carve a deep valley,
canyon or gorge.
It takes thousands of years
– or millions!

Making caves

Deep underground, there are damp, dark caves, hollowed out by water.

The water runs through cracks in the ground, and slowly dissolves limestone rock.

The cracks turn into caves, tunnels, passageways and rooms.

Water drips down, leaving tiny bits of dissolved rock behind. Slowly, it builds up into weird shapes.

31

MADE OF STONE

We use rocks and minerals to make all kinds of stuff. Look around a town, street or garden and you'll see them everywhere.

Stone dug from the ground becomes bricks for houses.

Concrete is made using rocks and sand.

Metals come from rocks too.

Glass is made of sand, mixed with minerals and melted.

Marble can be carved into statues.

Computer chips are made of silicon. It's a mineral that comes from sand.

THE STONE AGE

If you're lucky, when you're looking for pebbles you might find something like this.

This doesn't look like a natural pebble – and it's not. Thousands of years ago, someone shaped it. They chipped away at it with other stones to make a stone arrowhead.

Long ago, people didn't know how to make metal or plastic. They had to make things they needed from stone. They made stone weapons, furniture, jewellery and tools.

We now call that time the
Stone Age.

Stone Age people often made stone circles, like this.

What were they for? We don't know!

In Orkney, Scotland, there is a Stone Age village, called Skara Brae. There you can see Stone Age people's stone beds, shelves and fireplaces.

A STONE BONE

What if you find a pebble that looks like part of an animal? Maybe it is!

Long ago, animals died,
and their bodies quickly rotted away.

Hard parts, like bones, shells and beaks,
were left behind.

Sometimes, they got covered in sand and mud.
It got squashed down and became hard rock.

The body parts inside the rock slowly
dissolved away. Over time, minerals filled in the gaps.

We can find these stony body parts by digging for
them...

or when rocks wear away, and they are revealed.

They are called fossils.

Fossil ammonite

Dinosaur tooth

Fossil fish
skeleton

Is it a fossil?

How can you tell if you've found a fossil?

It will have a particular shape,
like a seashell, claw or tooth.
It probably won't look like
a normal pebble.

There are also
fossil plants, footprints,
and even poos!

Fossil
footprints

Fossil plant

Fossil poo

37

GETTING IT OUT

There are rocks lying around all over the place. I just picked my pebble up from the stream.

Salt

Silver

Gold

But some of the rocks we need are deep underground. Some are precious and rare.

There are mines deep underground, with tunnels leading to the best places to find useful rocks.

Workers go down into the mines to collect things like...

salt, silver and gold.

38

Or, they dig useful rocks out of a **big hole** in the ground, called a quarry.

Quarry workers use giant trucks and diggers to pick up the rocks and carry them away.

Sometimes they use explosives to break the rock apart.

...BANG!

39

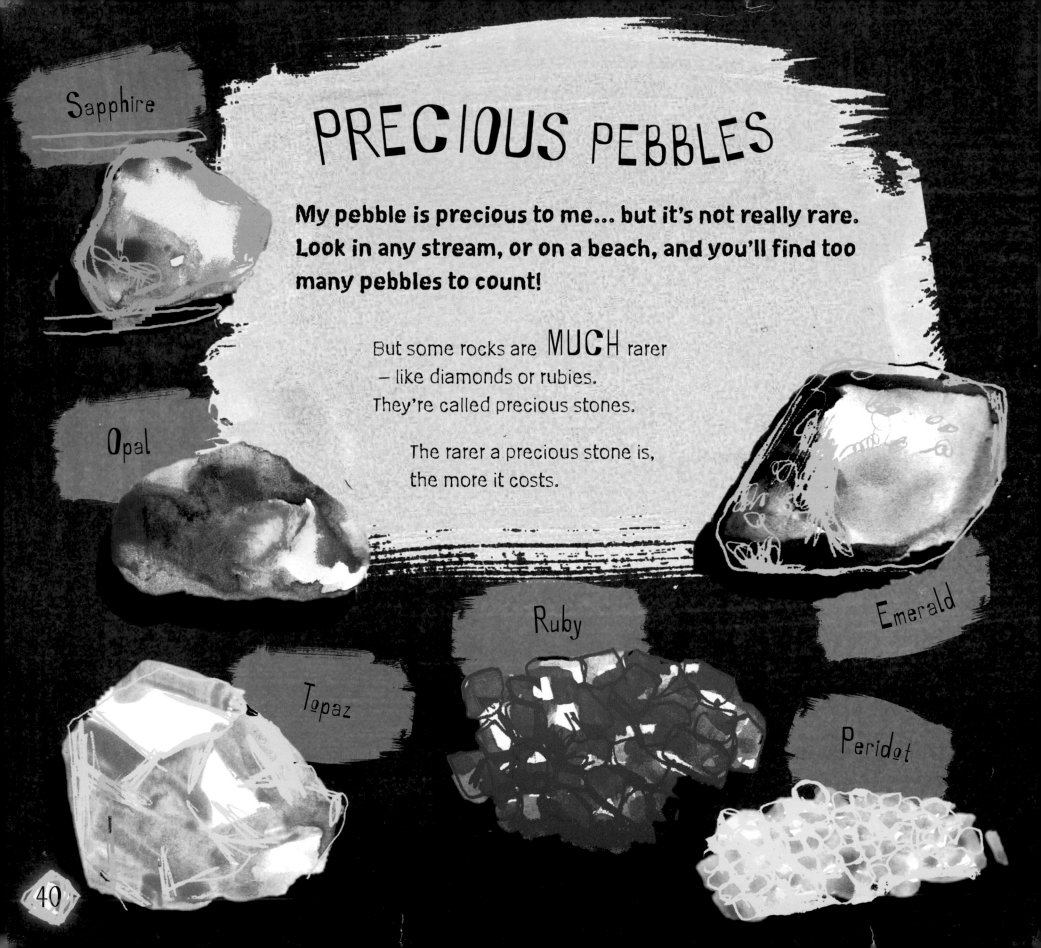

PRECIOUS PEBBLES

Sapphire

My pebble is precious to me... but it's not really rare. Look in any stream, or on a beach, and you'll find too many pebbles to count!

But some rocks are MUCH rarer
– like diamonds or rubies.
They're called precious stones.

The rarer a precious stone is,
the more it costs.

Opal

Emerald

Ruby

Topaz

Peridot

40

When a diamond comes out of the ground, it looks like a rough, see-through pebble.

It is carefully cleaned and cut into shape to make it sparkle.

Then it can be used to make a ring, or other jewels.

A diamond like this could cost more than a new house!

41

AMAZING PEBBLES

Some pebbles are just lumps of rock. Some are a bit stranger!

This pebble can hold up
a whole bunch of keys!
It's a natural magnet,
called a lodestone.

This is a desert rose.
It's not a flower, but a
strangely shaped rock,
that forms in sandy deserts.

This is a piece of a
clear mineral called
Iceland spar.
When you look through it,
it splits what you
can see into two,
so you see double.

If you found this pebble,
you might think you'd struck gold!
But it's a much more
common mineral, called pyrite.
It's also known as fool's gold,
as it has often tricked people
into thinking it is gold.

A PEBBLE OF MY OWN

My pebble isn't a precious diamond,
a mysterious magnet, or even a fossil.
It's just a plain, grey, oval pebble,
with a little white stripe. But there's
no other pebble exactly like it!

My pebble is very, very old.
It's from a time long
before houses or tents,
or even humans.
It waited all that time
for me to find it.

Maybe there are a million little grey pebbles in the world. Maybe there are a billion! And on other planets, stretching away into space, there are countless more pebbles.

But this one is my own special pebble, and I'm keeping it forever.

45

ACTIVITIES

Pebble skipping

You can throw a flat pebble across the still surface of a river or pond and make it jump or "skip".

   Hold the pebble in your fingers with one finger on the edge.

   Flick the pebble sideways with your wrist, using your finger to spin it as it goes.

   Aim to keep the pebble lying flat and close to the water surface.

(Make sure no one's in the way!)

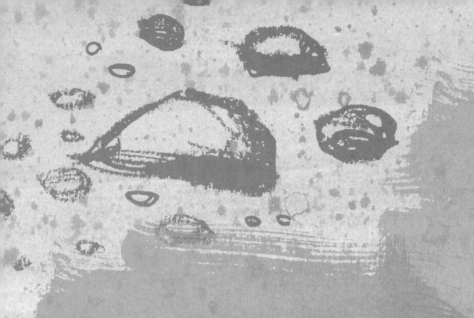

Pebble spotting

Look out for pebbles when you're outdoors. Can you find...

Pebbles with stripes, spots or speckles?

A pebble with a hole in?

A pebble that is perfectly round or egg-shaped?

Soft pebbles that you can use to draw on other pebbles or rock?

Flat pebbles?

See-through pebbles?

How many differently coloured pebbles can you collect?

Pebble art

Can you make a pebble sculpture by balancing pebbles in a tower? Or arrange them on the beach or the ground to make a pebble picture.

Pebble plates

If you collect some flat pebbles and fit them together, you can see how the Earth's plates work. Try pushing them around slowly.

GLOSSARY

arrowhead The sharp pointed end of an arrow. The earliest arrowheads were made of stone.

bedrock The layer of hard rock that lies underneath the soil.

boulder A big, heavy lump of rock.

computer chip The part inside a computer or smartphone that makes it work.

crust The layer of hard rock that covers the outside of the Earth.

eruption The time when hot melted rock or lava explodes or flows out of a volcano.

fossil A stone shape formed from the remains of a creature that lived long ago.

lava Hot melted rock or magma that has burst out from inside the Earth in a volcanic eruption.

magma The gooey, hot melted rock inside the Earth.

magnet A piece of rock or metal that can pull some types of metal towards it.

mine A set of human-made underground tunnels for getting useful rocks and minerals out of the ground.

mineral A pure material from the ground that is not mixed with other materials to form rock. Iron, diamond and silicon are examples of minerals.

plates The giant sections of rock that make up the Earth's crust, or hard surface.

quarry A hole in the ground or in a hillside where useful rock is dug out.

Stone Age Very long period of time that ended about 5,000 years ago. During this time, people used stone, bone, wood or horn to make tools. People had not yet discovered how to make metal or other materials.

INDEX